Bobby o

Helen Fuller Orton

Alpha Editions

This edition published in 2021

ISBN : 9789355342768

Design and Setting By
Alpha Editions
www.alphaedis.com
Email - info@alphaedis.com

As per information held with us this book is in Public Domain. This book is a reproduction of an important historical work. Alpha Editions uses the best technology to reproduce historical work in the same manner it was first published to preserve its original nature. Any marks or number seen are left intentionally to preserve its true form.

WHAT ROBIN REDBREAST KNEW

I

One cold morning in March, Bobby Hill was wakened by a sound he had not heard since last Fall, "Chirp, chirp, cheer-up."

"That sounds just like a robin," he thought.

He sat up in bed and looked out of the window. It was a cold, dark, stormy morning. Heavy clouds covered the sky. The North wind was blowing the snow hither and thither.

Bobby leaned nearer the window so he could see the ground. There was the snow like a blanket of white over the yard and the road and the fields. There were the snowdrifts like mountains and castles along the fences.

Bobby shivered as he looked at it and snuggled back under the covers.

"I must have been dreaming," he thought. "It isn't time for robins."

But he had no sooner settled down for another nap than he heard it again, "Chirp, chirp, cheer-up."

He got up and dressed quickly and went downstairs.

"Mother," he said, "I heard something that sounded just like a robin. What could it have been?"

"It *was* a robin," said Mother. "Come here and see him."

Bobby ran to the Big South Window. There on a branch of the maple tree was Robin Redbreast singing merrily.

"I thought the robins always stayed down South until Spring," said Bobby. "Why did he come back in the dead of Winter?"

"Spring is almost here," said Mother.

"Oh, indeed it can't be," said Bobby, "it is so cold and snowy."

"Robin knows," said Mother.

But Bobby looked out and saw the fields still covered with snow, and saw the huge snowdrifts like mountains and castles along the fences and the whirling snowflakes in the air, and thought, "Robin is mistaken this time."

After he had finished his morning chores, Bobby took his sled and slid down the little hill at the side of the house, as he had done nearly every day all Winter. Twenty-seven times he slid down the hill.

Then he and Rover, the Big Shepherd Dog, went across the field to the snowdrifts in the fence corners. Bobby slid down a huge snowbank, which gave his sled such a start that he went skimming over the field on the hard snow. Eight long slides he took there.

In the afternoon, he went skating on the Duck Pond. It was shiny and smooth and beautiful for skating. Twenty times across the pond he went.

When he went into the house, Mother said, "Well, Bobby, you have had a busy day."

"I've had lots of fun," said Bobby. "I shall go sliding and skating every day all Winter."

"That will not be long," said Mother.

"Oh, yes, it will," said Bobby. "Just see all the snow and ice."

If Bobby had only noticed, he would have known that even then the wind had changed to the south and it was becoming warmer. Soon the snow and ice began to melt. All night they kept melting.

The next day, Bobby was wakened again by Robin Redbreast. He looked out and saw the sun shining brightly. All that morning the snow melted so fast that by noon there were little rivers and pools of water everywhere.

Bobby tried to slide down the little hill; but there was a bare spot half way down, so his sled stuck on the ground and would not go any farther.

"This isn't any fun," thought Bobby. "I'll go over and slide down the snowbanks." He and Rover started across the field; but at every step they went down through the soft snow into the water beneath.

"This isn't any fun either. Is it?" said he to Rover.

Rover looked up into Bobby's face and seemed to say, "I don't care for it much myself." So they went back to the house.

Rover lay down by the fire to dry off; but Bobby took his skates and went to the Duck Pond. When he got there, he found the ice on the Duck Pond covered with pools of water.

"I'll wait till another day to skate," he thought.

He was just starting back to the house, when there came to his ears the same sound he had heard the last two mornings, "Chirp, chirp, chirp."

Bobby looked across the pond. There, on the ground under the willow tree, was a robin.

"Hello, Robin Redbreast," called Bobby. "I'm glad you are back again"

"Hello, Robin Redbreast," called Bobby. "I'm glad you are back again. But you'll be very cold up here. It isn't Spring yet."

"Chirp, chirp," said Robin. "Cheer-up, cheer-y." And he flew up to a branch of the willow tree.

Bobby's eyes followed Robin into the willow tree. What were all those little gray things on the twigs around Robin?

Bobby looked more closely. "Why I do believe—I do believe—can it be those are pussy willows?" he exclaimed.

Around the pond to the tree he ran. Sure enough! Pussy willows they were.

Bobby reached up and picked some of the twigs. Then he ran to the house as fast as he could run.

"Oh, Mother," he exclaimed, "see the pussy willows! I believe Spring *is* almost here."

"Robin knew," said Mother.

"Good!" said Bobby. Then he added, "But there won't be any more sleigh-rides, or sliding down hill, or skating."

"Just wait and see what fun Summer will bring," Mother replied.

II

The time of year had come when boys were flying kites. But around Cloverfield Farm no one had started yet.

Perhaps the little white clouds, floating in the sky, beckoned to Bobby, "Send a kite up to us, little earth boy."

Perhaps the wind, blowing in the tree tops, whispered, "Bring a kite and try me. Just see how far I will take it up for you."

Anyway, Bobby suddenly stopped playing and looked up into the sky. Then he ran into the house.

"I want to fly a kite," said he.

"I will help you make one," said Grandfather, who was visiting there.

Bobby hunted until he found the sticks and the string and the paper. Then they made a fine kite.

Mother helped, too. She made the paste of flour and water, and found bright strips of cloth for the tail. Then she wrote his name on the cross-stick— Bobby Hill.

Sister Sue went along to help him start it.

Up, up, went the kite into the sky.

"Ha, ha!" said Mr. Wind. "Here's some fun. I'll take that kite up to the clouds."

"Good!" said the little white clouds. "Here comes a kite to visit us."

"Up, up, went the kite into the sky"

It was not long before the cord was all unwound, and the kite looked like a speck against the sky.

"It must touch the clouds," said Bobby.

Mother came out on the porch to look at it. People driving along the road saw Bobby holding the string and looked up into the sky. "What a fine kite!" they said.

Mr. Hill had gone to the city that morning.

"You had better leave it up until Father comes home; he will want to see it," said Sue, as she started back to the house.

Neighbor Newman's boy saw Bobby's kite and went into his house to make one. Boys in the village saw it and began to make kites.

When it had been flying for some time, the wind began to blow harder, and the kite tugged and tugged on the string.

Suddenly, there was a strong gust of wind.

Snap went the string.

Away went the kite.

Bobby ran after it, to catch it when it fell. But it soon blew out of sight over the patch of woods. Then he sadly wound up the string that was left and went slowly to the house.

"My kite flew away," said he to Mother. "And it was the best one I ever had."

Meanwhile, the kite went sailing along.

"It's my kite," said the West Wind. And he tried to blow it toward the Little Red Schoolhouse.

"No, it's my kite," said the North Wind. And he tried to blow it toward the clouds.

In spite of them both, the kite began to fall. Zigzag it went, first one way, then another, across the road where the Little Red Schoolhouse stood, to an open field on the other side.

Mr. Hill was just coming home from the city on that road. As he was driving along, he saw the kite falling.

"Whoa, Prince," he said to the horse.

Prince stopped. Mr. Hill got out of the buggy and climbed over the fence. "Perhaps I can catch it," he thought. Just before he got to it, the kite came to the ground. Mr. Hill picked it up.

"What a fine kite!" he said. "I wonder what boy lost it. I'll inquire at the houses as I go along."

He wound up the string, gathered up all the tail and went back to the buggy. He started to put it under the seat; but as he did so, his eye fell on something written on the cross-stick. It was the name Mrs. Hill had written there—Bobby Hill.

"Well, well!" said he. "So it's Bobby's kite, is it?"

He put it under the seat, got into the buggy and drove toward home.

Father meant to give the kite to Bobby as soon as he reached home, but when he drove into the yard, there was a man waiting to see him on business; so he forgot all about it.

Bobby's big brother John unhitched Prince, put him into the stable and pushed the buggy into the carriage-house.

So there was Bobby's fine kite lying under the buggy seat, all unknown.

The next day, Grandfather helped Bobby make another kite. But perhaps it was not made of the right kind of wood, or the cross-piece was not at just the right place. Anyhow, it had not gone up far when it dived to the ground and was broken.

That evening Bobby told Father all about his kites. Then Father remembered something; but he said nothing about it just then.

The next morning, he called Bobby to him. "I have a present for you," he said. "Come to the carriage-house and you may see it."

"What is it like?" asked Bobby, as they walked along.

"It is something that flies," said Father.

"A bird," said Bobby.

"Wrong," said Father.

"A ball?" guessed Bobby.

"No. One more guess," said Father.

"I don't know anything else that flies," said Bobby, "except a butterfly."

"How about a bumblebee?" asked Father.

"Oh, Father, you couldn't catch a bumblebee," said Bobby. "And if you did, it would sting you."

"How about a kite?" asked Father.

"That would be grand," said Bobby. "Did you get one in the city?"

"Look under the buggy seat," said Father.

Bobby climbed into the buggy and reached under the seat and began to pull something out.

"Why, it looks just like the tail to my kite," said he.

"Why, it *is* my kite," he shouted, as he saw his name on the cross-piece. "Where did you get it?"

Father told him.

"I'll tie the string together and fly it again," said Bobby.

"You had better get some stronger cord," said Father. "I might not happen to find it if it flew away again."

Bobby rode to the village when John went to the blacksmith shop. He went to Mr. Brown's store and bought a ball of strong cord. Then he ran all the way home with it, because he did not want to wait for the blacksmith to finish shoeing the horse.

And it wasn't long before Bobby's kite had climbed high into the sky again.

People driving along the road saw it and said, "What a fine kite!"

Father saw it this time.

As he was going down the lane, he stopped a few moments to watch it. Then he waved his hand to Bobby and started on.

"I am glad it flew across my path," he said.

III

In the Spring, at Cloverfield Farm, all the family made gardens and sowed seeds.

Mother sowed pansy seed in a round bed in the side yard. When the little plants came up, she watered them and weeded them and kept the ground soft and fine, so they could grow.

All the time she was tending them, she kept thinking, "How nice it will be to have all these lovely pansies to look at this Summer!"

Father sowed some radish seed in the garden. When the little plants came up, he weeded them and hoed them and kept the ground soft and fine, so the little radish plants could grow.

All the time he was doing it, he was thinking, "How fine it will be to have lots of good radishes for the table!"

Bobby had a little corner all his own in Father's big garden. He sowed some onion seed in his garden. When the little plants came up, he weeded them and hoed them and kept the ground soft and fine, so they could grow.

All the time he was doing it, he was thinking, "How nice it will be to have all these onions, so I can give them to Mother for the cooking!"

One day, while the family were all away, the Old Brown Hen, who had stolen her nest, came along with her thirteen chickens.

She was hunting for a good place to scratch and find something for them to eat.

First, she tried to scratch in the gravel driveway, but that was too hard.

Next, she tried to scratch by the wood-pile, but the ground was covered with little chips, so she could not scratch there.

Then she found Mother's pansy bed. The ground in it was so soft that it was beautiful for scratching.

So she called, "Cluck, cluck, cluck!" and her thirteen chicks came running, and she scratched all over the pansy bed, to find bugs and worms for them to eat.

And all the little pansy plants were scratched up.

Next, she went over to the big garden and found Father's radish bed. The ground in it was so soft that it was a fine place for scratching.

So she called, "Cluck, cluck, cluck!" and her thirteen chicks came running, and she scratched all over the radish bed, to find something for them to eat.

And all the little radish plants were scratched up.

One would think that the Old Brown Hen would not have needed to scratch any more. But it takes a great deal to feed thirteen hungry, growing chicks.

So she kept hunting for other places to scratch; and it was not long before she found Bobby's onion bed.

Now Bobby had hoed in it and dug in it so much just the day before, that it was *very* soft and just beau-ti-ful for scratching.

"What good luck!" thought the Old Brown Hen. "A finer place for scratching I never saw."

"Cluck, cluck, cluck!" she called; and her thirteen chicks came running, and she scratched all over the onion bed, to find something for them to eat.

And all the little onion plants were scratched up.

Then, because they had eaten all they wanted, she wallowed in the soft earth until she had made a nice, comfortable place to sit.

There she sat, in the middle of Bobby's onion bed, and the thirteen chicks went under her wings to have a mid-day nap.

The Old Brown Hen went to sleep, too.

Soon the family came home. As they drove into the yard, Mother spied her pansy bed and cried, "Somebody has been digging in my garden and has dug all my little pansy plants up."

Next, they came to the big garden, and when Father saw his radish bed, he said, "Somebody's been digging in my garden and has dug all my radish plants up."

Then Bobby ran to look at his garden. When he saw it, he cried, "Somebody's been digging in my garden and here she is fast asleep."

When the Old Brown Hen heard Bobby shout, she woke up and ran away.

And her little chicks ran in all directions and called, "Peep, peep, peep!"

"Let's catch her," said John.

"When he saw it he cried, 'Somebody's been digging in my garden and here she is fast asleep'"

Father and John and Bobby chased the Old Brown Hen and caught her and put her in a chicken coop.

Then she called, "Cluck, cluck, cluck!" and her thirteen chicks came running.

And there they lived until the chicks were grown up.

And they did not scratch up any more gardens that Summer.

And that is the end of the story of the Old Brown Hen.

IV

One morning in May, Bobby saw the flock of sheep going along the gravel driveway toward the road.

Rover and Bobby's big brother John were driving them. Hobson, the hired man, went ahead.

"Where are you taking the sheep?" asked Bobby. "Have you sold them?"

"Come and you shall see," answered Father. "Do you want to ride with me in the buggy, or help drive the sheep?"

"I'd like to help," said Bobby.

"Well, here is a long stick for you," said Father.

Bobby was off like the wind and soon caught up with the others.

The leader of the flock, the big bell wether, went ahead. All the other sheep followed. Sometimes they tried to stop and eat grass by the roadside. Bobby was after them with his long stick.

Sometimes they tried to go into a farmer's yard. Rover chased them back into the road.

Once a big, black dog came from a farmyard, barking savagely. "Bow-wow, bow-wow!" he said. The sheep were dreadfully frightened. Some ran up the road and some ran down the road.

Rover ran at the big, black dog and drove him back into his yard. Then he and John and Hobson and Bobby brought the frightened sheep together again and started them down the road.

"I wonder where we are taking the sheep," thought Bobby.

About ten o'clock, they came to a creek with a bridge over it. Across the bridge they drove the sheep. On the other side, Hobson stopped them and drove them to one side of the road. Farmer Hill tied Prince to the fence.

"Can you guess what we came for?" he asked.

Bobby looked all around. John and Hobson and Rover were driving the sheep into a pen at the edge of the creek. The pen was surrounded by a fence of rails, with a gate near the water.

Then the men put on the old clothes which they had brought in the buggy, and went into the pen among the sheep.

Bobby looked puzzled.

"Let's take the bell wether first," said Mr. Hill; and John grabbed the old sheep in spite of his ugly-looking horns.

They took him through the gate and started to pull him toward the water.

"Oh, Father, I know," shouted Bobby. "You are going to wash the sheep."

When Bobby found that he had guessed right, he danced for joy. Then he settled down to see how it would be done.

Old Bell Wether was the largest sheep in the flock and had long, curved horns. He had been washed every year of his life, but he never liked to be dragged into the water. Now he held back with all the strength of his four stout legs.

John was in front, trying to pull him along. Farmer Hill and Hobson were behind, trying to push him along.

Suddenly, Old Bell Wether changed his mind. He lowered his head and rushed forward, striking John a tremendous blow.

Into the water went John. Bobby could not see a bit of him.

Into the water, too, went Old Bell Wether. But his head was above water and was moving out into the creek.

Bobby could not move or speak. He feared that big brother John would be drowned.

Then he saw John rising out of the water and Father helping him back to land.

"Old Bell Wether played us a sharp trick," said Mr. Hill.

"Oh, Father," shouted Bobby, "he is almost across the creek. He'll surely get away."

Farmer Hill was watching the pair of horns.

"We'll get him," said he.

He started toward the bridge, catching up a rope as he went. Hobson followed.

Before they could run across the bridge, Old Bell Wether walked up out of the creek and started toward home. But he was tired after his swim, and his wool was heavy with water.

They soon overtook him and drove him into a corner of the rail fence at the side of the road.

"Now we have you," said Farmer Hill, as he threw the rope over his horns.

"Before they could run across the bridge, Old Bell Wether walked up out of the creek and started for home"

Old Bell Wether had to submit and be led back over the bridge to the sheep-pen.

"You won't do that again, old boy," said John. "I'll be ready for you this time."

The men took him out into the water again. Keeping his head up so that he could breathe, they washed his long wool until it was quite clean.

Then they led him out of the water, into another sheep-pen, which had been built to hold the sheep after they were washed.

After all the sheep had been washed clean and white, they were started home again. When they were part way home, they met another flock of sheep coming down the road.

"Drive ours up next to the fence," said Farmer Hill, "so they will not get mixed with that flock."

So they were driven up by the fence and kept there until the other flock had passed on their way to be washed.

Bobby rode with Father in the buggy the rest of the way.

"How do they get the wool off the sheep?" he asked.

"That," said Father, "will be something more for you to see, another time. You won't have to wait many days."

Bobby had a great story to tell Mother and Sue that night.

V

A few days after the sheep had been washed at the creek, a strange man named Mr. Price came to Cloverfield Farm one morning.

"If you want to see something interesting," said Father to Bobby, "you may come along with us."

They all went down to the Old Red Barn, and Bobby noticed that the flock of sheep had been driven into the basement.

On the basement floor, near the gate which shut the sheep in their pen, they put down a platform of boards, about six feet square.

Then Mr. Price took several strange-looking things out of his bag.

"What is that?" asked Bobby, pointing to one of them.

"That is a pair of shears," said Mr. Price.

"They do not look like my Mother's shears," said Bobby.

"No, they don't," said Mr. Price. "But these are sheep-shears."

"Oh, I know," shouted Bobby, jumping up and down; "you are going to shear the sheep."

"Right, my boy," said the man. "Now keep your eyes open."

"You had better look out for Old Bell Wether," said Bobby. "He'll bunt you over, as he did John down at the creek."

"I've sheared thousands of sheep in my time," said Mr. Price, "and no sheep ever bunted me over yet."

The men brought out one of the smaller sheep through the gate, and tipped her over on her side, on the smooth boards. Mr. Price, bending over the sheep, began shearing off the wool close to the skin.

After he had sheared the wool from the upper side, he turned the sheep over and sheared the other side.

Bobby was watching with all his eyes.

When he had finished and the fleece lay flat on the platform, very white and clean, Mr. Price let the sheep get up and run out in the barn-yard.

"Ba-a-a—, Ba-a-a!" went the sheep, as she ran out, looking very small and feeling very strange with her heavy coat of wool gone.

Farmer Hill gathered up the wool and carried it to another part of the basement, while John and Mr. Price brought out the next sheep.

When Mr. Price had sheared four sheep, he said, "You might as well bring the big wether next."

"You must lose your wool, Mr. Bell Wether," said Bobby. "We need it to make our clothes."

"I think John had better help you hold him down," said Farmer Hill. "He is a cantankerous old fellow."

So John helped hold him, while Mr. Price sheared him.

Old Bell Wether was a wise old sheep. He knew he could not get away from two men. Besides, he was not sorry to lose the heavy coat which made him so warm in the hot Spring days.

Perhaps he knew that when a sheep squirms and kicks, the shearer may cut off a bit of the skin instead of just taking the wool.

At any rate, he lay very quiet until he was all sheared, and they let him run out into the yard.

"Oh, Father, Old Bell Wether didn't make a single bunt," shouted Bobby, bounding off to the place where Mr. Hill was taking care of the fleeces.

"Just see what I am doing," said Father.

Farmer Hill had a queer-looking thing made of boards joined together with hinges. It looked flat when he laid a fleece of wool on it. Then he folded it up until it looked like a box, and the wool was pressed together inside of it.

There were pieces of strong wool twine in grooves on the inside of the box. He tied them around the fleece so as to hold it firmly together.

At last he opened the box and out came a solid fleece of wool, in the shape of a cube about eighteen inches on each side.

"Oh, let me feel of it," said Bobby. He pressed his hands and face against the soft white wool.

"How much do you guess it weighs?" asked Mr. Hill, as he put it on the scales.

"Fifty pounds," said Bobby.

"Too much. Eight and a half," said Father, as he put the number down in a book.

"How do they make the wool into clothes?" asked Bobby.

"It is first spun into yarn," said Father. "Do you remember the old spinning wheel we have up in the attic?"

"Oh, yes," said Bobby. "That is what I turn my buzz-saw with."

"Well," said Father, "your grandmother used that wheel to spin yarn from wool like this."

"And then they knit stockings from the yarn," said Bobby.

"Yes," said Father; "but my grandmother used to weave the yarn into cloth on a loom. And she made the cloth into clothes for her children to wear."

"I wish Mother would spin yarn and make clothes," said Bobby.

"We find it cheaper to sell the wool and buy our clothes," said Father.

"And perhaps Mother has enough to do," said Bobby.

Then they went back to get another fleece.

When the sheep were all sheared, Rover drove them down the long lane to their pasture.

And it was not long before the whole flock were once more nibbling grass in the meadow.

VI

The proudest creature on Cloverfield Farm was Red Top, the big rooster.

He was called Red Top because of his beautiful, big red comb.

Red Top was proud of his big red comb. He was proud of his glossy reddish-brown feathers. He was proud of his crow.

"Just hear those silly hens," he would say. "All they can do is to cackle. But listen to my beautiful song. Cock-a-doodle-doo, cock-a-doodle-doo! Was there ever a grander sound?"

Every morning, on his perch in the hen-house, he would waken and crow before the break of day. Then he would go out in front of the hen-house and crow three or four times.

But the place he liked best for crowing was a little mound near the house. Farmer Hill's window was just above the little mound. John's window was near by.

Before they were awake, every morning in Summer, Red Top would go there and crow at the top of his voice.

Farmer Hill would waken and say, "There is Red Top. It is time to get up."

John would waken and say, "I wish Red Top would crow somewhere else."

Then there came a holiday when they did not need to get up so early. The evening before, Farmer Hill said, "I wish some one would keep Red Top from crowing under my window to-morrow morning, so I could sleep."

"I'll keep him away," said Bobby.

"You will have to watch or he will get there in spite of you," said Father.

"I don't believe you *could* keep him away," said John.

"You'll see that I can," said Bobby. "Red Top can't get the start of me."

"If you keep him from crowing there to-morrow morning," said John, "I will give you a dime."

"Goody! I'll do it," said Bobby. "I'll put the dime in the box for my new express wagon."

Bobby put the alarm clock near his bed. It was set to wake him at four o'clock.

The next morning, after Red Top had crowed in the hen-house, he went out into the yard and crowed three times. Then he started toward the house. Very proudly he strutted along the path.

He was just going around to the side of the house, when Bobby came out of the back door.

"Shoo, shoo!" said Bobby. "You must not crow near the house this morning."

And he drove Red Top back toward the corn crib.

"That is too bad," thought Red Top. "They will miss my nice crow. I must go again."

So he went up the path again toward the little mound. Bobby was watching and drove him back.

"I will not let you crow here this morning," he said. "Shoo, shoo!"

Six times Red Top tried to get to the little mound. Six times Bobby drove him back. Finally, he drove him beyond the horse barn.

"Crow for the walnut tree this morning," he said.

"He won't get to the house again very soon," thought Bobby. So he went over to the strawberry patch to see whether any strawberries were ripe.

Suddenly, in the apple tree, a robin began to sing. A thrush joined him from a near-by thicket. Birds began chirping in all the trees.

The Eastern sky began to turn golden. The fleecy white clouds began to look rosy.

Bobby forgot all about the rooster.

Soon there were birds singing everywhere—robins in the apple orchard, an oriole in the elm tree, swallows flashing through the farmyard, bluebirds and yellowbirds on every side. Bobolinks skimming over the clover field, joined the chorus.

Then on a low limb of the crab-apple tree, a meadow lark began to sing. Bobby tried to find him, but could not see him among the branches. Such a wonderful song he had never heard.

The Eastern sky was getting more rosy and more golden.

"It must be the sunrise that makes him so happy," thought Bobby. "I wish I could sing like that."

So there Bobby stood, golden sunrise in the East, singing birds around him.

Meanwhile, Red Top was quietly making his way to the house. As far as the wood-pile he came, and Bobby did not drive him back. As far as the pump he came.

"I'll soon be there," he thought.

A rooster in the next barn-yard crowed. Then Bobby remembered.

He ran toward the house. There was Red Top on the little mound.

"Oh, I must stop him before he crows," thought Bobby. He shouted, "Shoo, shoo!"

Just then a loud cock-a-doodle-doo rang out on the morning air.

"I beat you, Bobby," it seemed to say.

Father looked out of his window and said, "Red Top was smarter than you, wasn't he?"

"I am sorry I let him wake you," said Bobby.

John put his head out of his window and called, "You have lost the dime, Bobby."

"I don't care," said Bobby. "I heard the birds and saw the sunrise."

Then he chased Red Top down to the Old Red Barn, so Father could finish his morning nap.

VII

One of the many pretty sights on the farm in early June, was the clover field, all covered with red blossoms.

It was an interesting place, too.

Bobby and Rover loved to romp in it. The honey bees came to it to get honey. The bobolinks, like flashes of black and white, skimmed over it as they sang. The ground-birds had their nests in it.

Bobby knew of three nests there.

But the time had come for cutting the clover.

One morning, Bobby saw Father and Hobson in the tool-shed and went to see what they were doing. He found them busy about the mowing-machine—oiling it, tightening the screws and sharpening the knives.

"Oh, Father, you aren't going to cut the grass now, are you?" said Bobby.

"Yes," said Father, "the clover is ready."

"I wish it could be left all Summer," said Bobby.

"But we must cut it," said Farmer Hill, "to make hay for the horses and cows to eat next Winter."

When the mower was ready, they hitched Prince and Daisy to it, and Father climbed to the seat and drove to the hayfield.

As the mower went around the field, it cut a wide swath of clover and left it lying flat on the ground.

A humming sound the mower made, a pleasant sound to a person some distance away, a very loud sound to one near by.

In one of the nests in the field, there was a mother bird and three young birds. The little mother bird, there in the quiet clover field, had never heard such a loud sound before.

"What can it be that makes that big noise?" the frightened mother bird thought as the mower passed close by.

Then the sound grew fainter as the mower went to the other side of the field. The little mother bird settled down happily in her nest.

But it was not long before the sound came back again, closer and louder than before.

"What shall I do?" thought the mother bird. "What shall I do?"

She might have flown away herself. But there were the three young birds not yet old enough to fly.

So she sat still while the terrible noise kept coming nearer.

All this time, Bobby was playing here and there with Rover. Suddenly, Bobby thought of something. He ran toward the mowing-machine, waving his hands and shouting.

"Stop, Father, stop!" he said.

The mower made such a loud noise that Father could not hear what Bobby was saying, but he could see his arms waving.

"Whoa, Prince! Whoa, Daisy!" he said, and the horses stopped.

"What is the matter, Bobby?" he asked.

"'Stop, Father, stop!' he said"

"The bird's-nest! There's a nest right ahead," shouted Bobby.

"A bird's-nest, is there?" said Father. "Well, we won't harm the nest. Go and stand near it, Bobby, and I'll turn out for it."

Bobby hunted around until he found it in the clover. Then he took his stand beside it.

Father clucked to the horses. "Get-up, Prince! Get-up, Daisy!" he said. When he came near Bobby, he turned out and passed a few feet away, leaving the nest all safe.

Bobby stood there until Father went around the field and came back again, so that the wheels of the mower would not run over the nest or the horses step on it when passing on the other side.

"Are there any more nests in the field?" asked Father.

"There is one at that end," said Bobby, pointing toward the west; "and one down there," pointing toward the east.

"If you will set a tall stick in the ground near each one," said Mr. Hill, "I can see where the nests are, and you won't have to stand there."

"All right," said Bobby, and he started toward the house for the sticks.

As he was hunting for them, he remembered his little flags that always stood in the corner of the parlor.

"Why not use the flags to keep the bird's nests safe?" he thought.

So he ran into the parlor, took three of the flags and ran back to the clover field.

In the nest at the western end of the field were four little birds. Bobby pushed one of the sticks into the ground beside it, and the flag floated in the breeze.

Away to the other end of the field he ran, to the nest where there were two little birds. He planted one of the sticks in the ground beside it, and that flag floated in the breeze.

Then he went to the nest where he had stood guard. "You shall have a flag, too," he said.

Farmer Hill kept driving around the field, cutting the clover. But when he came near a flag, he turned out and left a patch of clover standing around the nest.

The sun shone brightly and dried the clover. The breezes blew over it and dried it. Together they changed it from fresh grass into sweet-smelling hay.

The next day, John hitched Daisy to the hay-rake and drove it up and down the field, raking the hay into long windrows.

The hired men came with their pitchforks and pitched it into little stacks or haycocks.

But they were all careful not to touch the little patches of clover where the flags flew.

People driving along the road wondered why Farmer Hill had left the three little patches of clover standing and why the three little flags were there.

But the three little mother birds knew and were happy.

ON TOP OF THE WORLD

VIII

For a few days, Bobby and Betty and Rover had fun playing hide-and-seek among the haycocks.

"Well, Bobby," said Father one morning, "can you and Betty spare the hay, so we can draw it into the barn?"

"Oh, no; we want to play in it some more," said Bobby.

"We must put it into the barn before a rain comes," said Father. "Come down to the field, you and Betty. Perhaps there will be some fun to-day."

Prince and Daisy were hitched to the big lumber wagon. Father and Hobson took the wagon box off and put the wide hay-rack on.

"Come, children, climb up on the rack for a ride to the field," said Father.

Father held Betty; but Bobby, sitting in the bottom of the rack, went jigglety, jigglety, shakety, shake.

And wasn't it fun!

When they came to the field, Father helped the children off. Then he drove along beside a haycock and stopped the horses. Hobson pitched the hay onto the rack with his pitchfork. Father placed the hay around, so the load would be even on both sides. Then he drove on and stopped at the next haycock.

Higher and higher the load grew.

"Look at Father, Betty," said Bobby. "He is almost up to the sky."

When the load was high enough, Father called to Hobson, "That will do."

In the middle of the load, Father pushed the hay aside to make a nest. A very big nest it was, too big for a robin, too big for the old brown hen.

Then he called down, "Bobby, how would you and Betty like to ride to the barn on the load of hay?"

"That would be grand," said Bobby; "but we can't get up there."

Father said to Hobson, "I'm ready for the children now."

Hobson lifted Bobby to the foot of the little ladder which is at the front of a hay-rack. Bobby climbed up the ladder and Father reached down and pulled him up to the top of the load.

"Here's a safe place for you," said Father, as he put Bobby in the big nest.

Then Hobson lifted Baby Betty. "You had better bring her all the way up," said Father. "She is too little to climb the ladder."

Hobson carried her up the ladder and put her in the nest.

"You may drive," said Father to Hobson. "I'll stay with the children." So there they were in the nest, Father and Bobby and Betty, on top of the big load of hay.

All the way up the lane they rode.

"We must be close to the sky," said Bobby.

"We're on top of the world," said Father.

Finally, they came to the Red Barn. The big front doors were open. Very wide and high they were, but the load of hay reached almost to the top.

"We must all scooch down," said Father, "or it will strike us."

So they all bent over flat on the hay, while Prince and Daisy drew them safely into the big barn.

"Now we must climb down the ladder," said Bobby.

"Wait a minute," said Father. "Sit quietly until I call you."

Father climbed down.

"Ready, Hobson," he called.

Hobson took Bobby over to the side of the load. There was Father standing below him, waiting with outstretched arms.

"Slide down, Bobby; I'll catch you," said Father.

Down the side of the load of hay slid Bobby, straight into Father's arms.

Then it came Betty's turn.

"It's so high," she said. "I'm 'fraid."

"Don't be scared; I'll catch you," said Father.

"Father'll catch you," called up Bobby.

Betty took courage.

Down she slid, down the side of the load of hay, straight into Father's arms.

After that load was pitched into the hay-mow, they went for another, and then another, all day long.

Every time, Bobby and Betty rode in the nest on top of the load of hay.

BOBBY FORGETS

IX

In a chicken coop in the back yard at Cloverfield Farm, lived Old Speckle with her ten chickens.

It was Bobby's duty to feed them. Three times a day—morning, noon and night—he would take the basin of corn meal and water which Mother had stirred up, and would throw it by spoonfuls into the coop for the chickens.

Old Speckle would call, "Cluck, cluck, cluck!" and the ten little chicks would come running to eat.

He would throw some corn or wheat in for Old Speckle.

One morning Mother said, "Here is the breakfast for the chickens, Bobby."

"I'll feed them right away," said Bobby.

And he meant to.

Taking the basin of meal in one hand and the basin of wheat in the other, he started toward the chicken coop.

When he was about half way there, he spied his new white rabbit poking her nose out between the slats of the rabbit-pen.

Bobby stopped. For a few moments he stood and watched her. Then he set the two basins down on the ground and went over to the rabbit-pen.

"I'll be back in a minute," he said to himself. "It won't hurt the chickens to wait a little while for their breakfast."

Bunny was so interesting with her long ears and her wiggly nose, that Bobby stayed fifteen minutes, watching her. By that time, he had forgotten all about Old Speckle and the chickens.

Next he went to a corner of the rail fence to see whether there were any more eggs in the robin's nest. He found four blue eggs.

Then to the Duck Pond he went to see whether the little boat he had left there the day before was still there. It was. He sailed it eleven times across the pond.

When he was through sailing the boat, he saw Rover coming through the orchard.

"Hello, Rover," he said, "let's go to the barn."

And they went down the lane to the Big Red Barn, leaving Old Speckle and the ten little chicks still unfed.

"Why doesn't Bobby come with our breakfast?" thought the hungry little chicks.

"Why doesn't Bobby come with our breakfast?" thought Old Speckle. "My poor little chicks will starve."

Meanwhile the Big Rooster found the basin of meal and the basin of wheat.

"What a nice breakfast!" he thought.

And he ate it all up.

When noon time came, the dinner bell rang.

"Come, Rover," said Bobby. "Let's go up to dinner right away. It's a long time since breakfast."

Perhaps it was because he was hungry that Bobby suddenly remembered something.

Anyway, he began to run as fast as his legs would carry him and ran all the way up the lane, Rover at his heels.

And, as he ran, he kept thinking, "A long time since breakfast! But the little chickens didn't have any breakfast at all."

When he came to the spot where he had left the two basins, there the two basins were, but both empty.

He looked over toward the chicken coop.

There was Old Speckle walking back and forth, putting her head out between the slats every once in a while, and looking greatly distressed.

There were the little chicks saying, "Peep, peep, peep," as they tried to find something to eat in the grass.

Bobby took the basins into the house.

"Mother," he asked, "did you feed the chickens?"

"No," said she, "that is your chore, Bobby."

"But how came the basins empty?" asked he.

Mother could not answer. But at that very moment, the Big Rooster crowed, "Cock-a-doodle-doo! I had a fine breakfast."

Mother stirred up another basin of meal while Bobby got some more wheat. He took them quickly to the chickens and threw the food into the coop.

"Cluck, cluck, cluck!" Old Speckle called.

"Peep, peep, peep!" cried the little chicks, as they came running to eat.

Bobby watched them until it was nearly gone.

"Now you feel better, don't you?" said he. "And I feel better, too," he added.

Which was strange, wasn't it?

For Bobby had not yet had his dinner.

ROVER GOES TO THE STORE

X

Rover was useful in many ways about the farm. Sometimes he even went to the village store on errands.

One morning in Summer, Mrs. Hill needed some meat for dinner. She wrote a note and put it in a certain basket. With it she put a purse and covered them with a white cloth. Then she went to the door and called, "Rover! Rover!"

Rover came bounding up the path.

"I want you to go to the store," said Mrs. Hill, giving him the basket.

Rover took the handle in his mouth, trotted down the path to the road and turned toward the village. As he passed the Allen farmhouse, he saw Sport, a little brown dog with whom he often played.

Sport came running out with a few friendly barks which meant, "Come on, Rover, I am ready for a frolic."

Rover turned his head toward his little friend, but kept trotting right on, with a look that plainly said, "I can't stop to play now. I'm on important business."

When he came to Mr. Brown's store, there were some men standing on the steps.

"Well, Rover," said one of the men, "what did you come for to-day?"

Rover looked at the man, but walked right on, pushed the screen door open and went into the store.

"Good morning, Rover," said Mr. Brown. "What can I do for you?"

Rover put the basket on the floor and then looked up. Mr. Brown took out the white cloth and found the note Mrs. Hill had put there.

"Two pounds of beefsteak. Very well," said he.

He weighed a piece and wrapped it with paper and put it in the basket. Out of the purse he took a bill and put some change back.

Then he covered them with the white cloth and put a brown wrapping paper on top, to keep out the dust.

"You can take this home now, and mind you don't lose it," said he, as he held the door open.

Rover took up the basket and went down the steps.

"A pretty smart dog!" said one of the men, as Rover trotted along.

Down the street he went, with the basket held high from the ground.

Rover could smell the meat, and it made him feel hungry. But he had never touched anything that he carried in his basket and he did not do it now.

When he came to the house where Ned Hopkins lived, he saw Ned sitting on the fence, whittling a stick.

"I'll try to make Rover drop that basket," said Ned. He whistled and called, "Here, Rover, get it," as he threw the stick across the road.

Rover stopped and looked longingly at it. One of his favorite games was to fetch sticks that were thrown for him. But he did not run after it this time.

"Come, Rover, old dog," said Ned, getting down from the fence; "let me see what is in your basket." He patted Rover on the neck and then reached over to take the basket.

Rover held the handle tightly in his teeth and growled, "Gr-r-r-"

Ned had never heard Rover growl like that before.

"Oh, well, if that is the way you feel about it, I won't bother you," said he.

"Gr-r-r! You had better not," growled Rover. And he started on up the road.

After leaving the village, he came to a house where a man named Mr. Hook lived all alone. Mr. Hook was sitting in his front yard as Rover came along.

"I wonder what is in the basket to-day," he thought.

"Rover, old dog, wait a minute," he called.

Rover stopped and looked around. The basket felt quite heavy by this time, so he was glad to set it down on the ground.

Mr. Hook came up and patted him on the head. "Nice old dog! Nice Rover," he said. "What is in your basket?"

He put out his hand to take it. But Rover seized the handle and started toward home.

Mr. Hook looked up and down the road. There was no one in sight.

"Here, Ponto! Come, Ponto!" he called; and his own dog came running out—a big, black dog.

"Get him, Ponto," said the man.

Ponto ran after Rover and attacked him savagely. Rover had to put the basket down, to defend himself.

Ponto soon found he was getting the worst of it and turned to run.

Rover chased him down the road, leaving the basket alone on the ground. That was exactly what Mr. Hook wanted. He went quickly up to it and lifted the paper and the white cloth.

"Just what I thought!" he said to himself. "That would taste pretty good for dinner. The dog won't know the difference."

He reached down to take the beefsteak out.

But Rover had finished chasing Ponto and was on the way back. When he saw the man reaching into his basket, he ran back as fast as he could go.

"Bow-wow! bow-wow!" he barked. He looked so big and savage, and he barked and growled so loud, that Mr. Hook dropped the meat back into the basket. But he did not wait to put the white cloth and the brown paper over it.

Rover took the basket up and walked swiftly toward home. Mr. Hook stood looking after him and thinking, "I wish that dog were not so big and savage."

Bobby was waiting for Rover under the maple tree in the front yard, and they walked to the house side by side.

As Rover set the basket on the floor, Mrs. Hill picked it up and said, "I wonder why the meat is on top of the cloth and the paper."

But Rover did not tell.

XI

"Quack, quack, quack!" said the Big White Duck, as he started down to the Duck Pond below the orchard.

"Quack, quack, quack!" said the six other ducks, as they fell in line behind the leader.

"Let's all a-swimming go," they said.

And away they all went, waddling along in a procession, one behind another.

But when they got there, the Duck Pond was dry.

"It is very strange," thought the ducks. "What has happened to our pond?"

But all they said was, "Quack, quack, quack!" as they walked on the dry earth where the water had been.

Before long the leader started back toward the farmyard.

So all the ducks fell in line and waddled back, one behind another. They drank from the tub of water at the pump, but they could not swim in it because it was too small, and so they could not keep their feathers clean and white.

Now this is why the Duck Pond was dry.

For weeks there had been no rain at Cloverfield Farm.

Every day the sun had shone brightly all day.

The ground was very dry. The grass was dead and brown. The cistern had become empty. In the road the dust was several inches deep.

"The plums and peaches are falling from the trees," said Farmer Hill. "If it doesn't rain soon, we won't have any fruit."

"My flowers are dying," said Mother.

They watched the sky every day, to see if there were any signs of rain.

"I see a little cloud," said Bobby every few days. "Perhaps it will rain to-day."

But the little cloud would float lazily across the sky and bring no rain.

Every day the ducks would go in a procession down to the Duck Pond to swim. Every day they would find the Duck Pond dry and come back, one behind another, and take a drink from the tub of water at the pump.

And so five weeks passed.

At last, one day, big clouds gathered in the sky.

Bobby saw them first and came running in to tell the news.

"It's going to rain," he shouted. "See the big, big clouds."

Mother and Sue went to the door and looked out.

"It's surely going to rain," they said.

"I'll help put the windows down," said Bobby. And he ran to do it.

The men stopped work and put the horses in the barn, so they would not get wet. The hens and chickens went under the shed. The cows in the pasture went under the big trees.

It was not long before the lightning flashed and the thunder crashed and the rain came down.

They all went to the Big South Window to watch the storm—Father, Mother, John, Sue, Bobby and Betty.

"I like to watch a storm," said Bobby.

"It is a good sight," said Father. "Now the corn and potatoes will grow and the fruit will stay on the trees."

"My flowers will blossom again," said Mother, "and we'll have water in the cistern."

"I hope it will make the grass green," said Sue.

"I hope it will fill the Duck Pond," said Bobby, "so I can sail my boats and the ducks can have a swim."

As they stood there, suddenly Bobby called out, "Oh, see the ducks!" There they were in the rain, waddling around in the pools of water.

"Quack, quack, quack!" said the Big White Duck. "Isn't this grand?"

"Quack, quack, quack!" said the six other ducks, as they shook their feathers and waggled their tails.

After the rain had stopped and the pools had begun to dry up, Bobby saw the Big White Duck start off toward the Duck Pond.

All the other ducks followed, one behind another.

Down to the Duck Pond they went and found it full of water.

So all the ducks a-swimming went and were content.

XII

The day after the big rain, Bobby and Rover were down at the Duck Pond.

Bobby would throw a stick out into the middle of the pond and shout, "Get it, Rover."

Rover would jump into the water, swim out to the stick and bring it back in his mouth. Nine times Bobby threw the stick into the pond. Nine times Rover brought it back.

When they had done that long enough, Rover shook himself to get the water out of his coat, and lay down on the bank to dry.

Bobby spied an old raft, lying at one edge of the pond, under the willow tree. "I'll play on the raft," he thought.

It was only a few days since Mother had said, "Never go on the raft, Bobby, unless Father or John is at the pond with you."

"Oh, pshaw!" thought Bobby. "There is no danger; I'll have a little fun."

For some time he was content to keep near the shore, just pushing the raft around a little with a long pole. Then, growing bolder, he thought, "I'll go clear across the pond. Mother will never find it out."

So across the pond he started. Near the middle the water was deeper, so he had to go to the edge of the raft and lean over to make his pole touch bottom.

A little farther, and a little farther, he leaned. The raft began to tip and the first thing Bobby knew, he went head first into the water.

Down he went, to the bottom of the pond.

When he came up, he was lucky enough to be near the raft, and he grabbed the edge of it.

"Help! help!" he shouted. He tried to climb up on the raft but could not do it.

No one heard him shout, except the ducks that were swimming not far off. They said, "Quack, quack, quack!" but they could not help him.

Rover, over on the bank, was dozing in the sun. The first time Bobby called, Rover wiggled his ears but went on dozing.

Bobby shouted again, "Help! help!"

Rover heard this time and stood up and looked out over the water.

He saw Bobby clinging to the raft. Into the water he jumped and swam as fast as he could.

When he came near, Bobby said, "Oh, Rover, can't you help me out?" He took hold of Rover's collar with his right hand but still clung to the raft with his left hand.

Rover tried to swim toward the shore but the raft was so heavy he could not go very fast. So Bobby let go of the raft and then Rover could pull him along.

Bobby clung to Rover's collar until they reached shallow water.

"I'm glad you were near, Rover," he said, when they were on dry ground.

"Bobby clung to Rover's collar until they reached shallow water"

Bobby did not want to go to the house and tell Mother what had happened, but there was no other way.

So Bobby, all wet and drippy, and Rover, all wet and drippy, went to the house together.

"Why Bobby Hill, what have you been doing?" asked Mother, when she saw his wet, muddy clothes.

When he told her about getting on the raft she looked surprised. When he told her what Rover did, she turned and patted Rover's neck and said, "Good dog, good dog!"

"Of course, you will have to go to bed while your clothes get dry," she said to Bobby.

"Can't I put on one of my clean suits?" he asked.

"No," said Mother. "When boys get on rafts and fall into the water, they always go to bed while their clothes dry."

So to bed Bobby went in the middle of the day.

Mother washed his clothes and hung them to dry in the shade of the apple tree.

Sue tied a blue ribbon on Rover's collar, and Mother gave him a plate of cold roast beef with potatoes and gravy.

XIII

Of all the horses on Cloverfield Farm, Prince was the one the children liked best.

Prince would take a lump of sugar from Bobby's hand and not bite him. He would let Bobby and Betty come near and not kick them.

Sometimes Bobby rode on Prince's back, very slowly, with Father walking along beside.

"When shall I be allowed to go trotting down the road all alone, like John and Sue?" asked Bobby.

"Not until you are older," answered Father.

One day Bobby was down in the field where Hobson was working. When the dinner bell rang, Bobby said, "Let me ride Prince up to the barn."

"You might fall off," said Hobson. "I think I had better not let you."

"I can hang on," said Bobby. "Father lets me ride sometimes."

Hobson thought a moment. "All right; if you'll be careful, I'll let you ride this time," he said.

He let Daisy go on ahead, and then lifted Bobby to Prince's back with the big, clumsy work harness still on.

"Hold on tight and go slow," said he, as he gave Bobby the check rein.

Through the gap into the lane went Daisy, up the lane toward the barn. Prince and Bobby followed.

When Father let Bobby ride up to the barn, he always walked along beside. But after Hobson had started them off, he went across lots to the barn.

So there was Bobby riding Prince all alone.

How big and grand he felt!

When they were part way up the lane, Daisy, who was in a hurry for her dinner, began to trot.

"Let us trot, too," said Bobby. "Get-up, Prince."

Prince was hungry and thirsty. So when Bobby said a second time, "Get-up, Prince," and pulled on the check rein, Prince began to trot.

Father was in the farmyard at the head of the lane, fixing the drill for the wheat sowing.

"Bobby felt happy and grand. Prince felt happy and grand"

"I can ride as well as John or Sue," thought Bobby. "I'll show Father I can."

Up and down, up and down, he bounded as Prince trotted along.

Prince was enjoying it too.

"I'll give Bobby a good ride," he thought. And he arched his neck and trotted proudly up the lane.

Bobby felt happy and grand.

Prince felt happy and grand.

Now along the sides of the lane, there were thistle patches; and in one place near the head of the lane, there was a low stone pile with thistles growing up between the stones.

Bobby always kept away from thistle patches when he was barefoot.

They had gotten almost to the head of the lane, when Prince began to trot faster. Bobby bounded up and down higher than ever, his bare feet hitting the horse's sides at every step.

And then, the first thing he knew, he began to slide off.

"Whoa! whoa!" he shouted.

He grabbed a piece of the harness and tried to hold on, but at every step Prince took he slid farther.

"Whoa! whoa!" he shouted again.

Prince slowed up, but it was too late. He turned his head just in time to see Bobby tumble to the ground. Then he stopped stock still.

Down on the stones and the thistles Bobby fell.

This was bad enough, but then he rolled against Prince's hind foot, a little stunned by the fall.

Father saw Bobby fall and ran toward him, thinking as he ran, "Oh, what if Prince steps on Bobby or kicks him?"

And Father ran faster than he had ever run before.

But there Prince stood and kept his foot as still as still could be, until Father came and pulled Bobby away. Then Prince started on to the barn.

"Are you hurt?" asked Father.

"Not much," replied Bobby, as he rubbed his bruises.

Father helped him get the thistles out of his bare feet and legs. There were sixteen.

"That was a grand ride, though," said Bobby.

They went to the barn together and came up to Prince at the watering-trough.

Father took Prince's face in his two hands and in his kindest voice said, "You are a wonderful horse, Prince. Thank you for being careful of my Bobby. You shall have some extra oats to-day."

When Sue was told about it, she found another blue ribbon and tied it on Prince's bridle.

XIV

Mother's favorite place in all the house was by the big window in the sitting-room. It was on the south side of the house; so they called it the Big South Window.

On bright days the sun shone through it and flooded the sitting-room with golden sunshine. From it Mother could see green fields near by and purple hills in the distance and the blue sky over all.

"I love my Big South Window," she often said.

She sat there to do the sewing and mending. She sat there to read and sometimes just to enjoy the view—orchard and woods, green fields and the big elm tree, purple hills and blue sky.

One day in Autumn, a letter came to Mother from her sister. "Please come and make me a visit," the letter said.

"I do not see how I can go," said Mother. "There are so many things to be done here."

"Oh, yes, you must go," said Father. "You have not had a vacation in a long time. We'll get Aunt Martha to come and keep house."

"I'll look after the chickens and the ducks," said Bobby. "And I'll keep the wood box full for Aunt Martha."

So one day in October Mother said good-by and went away on her long journey. She was to be gone three weeks.

From the very first, Bobby missed her greatly. Most of all he missed her at evening, when she was not there to tell him a good-night story. But for the first week he stood it very well, his extra chores helping to pass the time away.

After that it seemed such a long time since he *had* seen her, and such a very long time until he *would* see her, that he could scarcely wait.

Every morning he counted the days until she would come home. When the second week had passed, he could say, "Only seven more days until Mother comes home."

That day, after he had fed the chickens and ducks and filled the wood box, he went into the sitting-room and sat in Mother's rocker and looked out through her favorite window.

Then he noticed how dirty it was.

"That will never do," thought Bobby. "Her window must be as bright and shiny as if she were here to look at it."

Bobby washed the big window on the inside and then he went outside. By standing on the kitchen stool and getting Aunt Martha to push down the upper sash, he could reach the top.

So with feeding the chickens and the ducks, and romping with Rover, and looking after Betty, and watching the men at work, and playing with his blocks and trains, and reading a book which Mother sent him, another week passed.

At last came the morning when it was only a few hours before she would come.

Bobby could hardly eat any breakfast for the joy of it.

All the forenoon, he and Sue were sweeping and dusting and putting the house in order.

Sue picked some pansies from Mother's pansy bed and put them in a dish on the dining table.

Bobby went to the fence corners and picked some beautiful red bitter-sweet for the sitting-room. Last of all, they washed the Big Window.

After dinner, to pass the time away, Bobby took his ball and began to bounce it on the side of the house.

"I'll see whether I can catch it a hundred times," thought he.

Ninety-seven times he caught it. "I'll soon have a hundred," he said. "Won't that be fine to tell Mother?"

He screwed up his mouth and threw the ball again. But instead of hitting the boards it hit the Big South Window.

Crash went the glass, in dozens of pieces, to the ground.

"Oh! oh!" moaned Bobby, as he stood looking at the ruined window.

"Why did I do it? Why *did* I do it?"

Sue heard the crash and came to see what had happened.

"It is too bad," said she.

"I must get another glass put in before Mother comes home," he said.

"There is not time," said Sue. "And probably there is not so large a pane without going to the city. But we can pick up the pieces and make it look as tidy as possible."

So they picked up the pieces, and Bobby carried them off to the barrel where they kept broken glass and dishes.

When Bobby had put the broken pieces of glass in the barrel, he went into the sitting-room. How ugly the Big Window looked now, with the big, jagged hole in it and the glass cracked in all directions. He felt the chill November air coming in through the broken pane.

"It will never do," thought he. "I must get a new pane put in right away."

He went to his bank, which was standing on the clock-shelf. In it he found four dollars, which he had been saving for a long time to buy a new Express Wagon.

"I hope it will be enough," he said.

There was only one man in the village who kept window glass—Mr. Barlow, the carpenter. As fast as he could run, Bobby ran to the village, and as he ran, he kept thinking, "Will he be at home? Will he have a big glass?"

When Bobby reached Mr. Barlow's shop, as soon as he could get his breath, he said, "Oh, Mr. Barlow, have you a big window pane? I've broken our Big South Window."

"Broken your Big South Window, have you? Well, that is too bad. I think I haven't one now, and to-morrow is Sunday; but I'll get you one on Monday when I go to the city."

"Oh, but it must be put in to-day," said Bobby. "I have the money to pay you. Would four dollars be enough?"

"I think that would be enough," said Mr. Barlow. "But I will have to nail boards over it to-night and get a big pane Monday."

"But I do so want it put in to-day," said Bobby. "Mother is coming home on the four o'clock train."

"So your mother's coming home, is she?" He saw the anxious look on Bobby's face.

"I will see what I can find," he said.

Mr. Barlow's shop was piled full of all sorts of things for building houses. Besides his work bench and tool chests, there were piles of lumber, bundles of shingles, odd window sashes and, in one corner, some window panes. He went to this corner and looked over the panes.

"No," he said, "there is nothing big enough."

Bobby began to look here and there. Back of a pile of lumber, he found two window panes.

"Here, Mr. Barlow," he called. "Here are some big ones."

"Well! well! I had forgotten them," said Mr. Barlow. He came back there and measured them. "Almost big enough," he said, "but not quite. I remember just the size of your big window. These lack three inches.

"I'm afraid you will have to wait, sonny," he added.

Bobby tried to keep back the tears, but they would come; he was so disappointed. Mr. Barlow thought a moment.

"I'll tell you what I'll do," said he. "I had some big windows taken over to Mr. Martin's new house this morning. He is going to have two windows just the size of yours. If they are not yet put in, I think Mr. Martin will let me take one for you and get him another next week."

Bobby and the carpenter went over to Mr. Martin's house. They found that one of the big panes had already been put in, and the man was just going to start on the other.

"Wait a minute," said Mr. Barlow. "We may not want that one put in to-day."

Then he said to Mr. Martin, "Will you let me put that big pane into Mr. Hill's window? I'll get another one for you on Monday."

"Why not get Mr. Hill's on Monday?" asked Mr. Martin.

"Well, you see, Bobby broke their big window and his mother is coming home to-day," said the carpenter.

"I see," said Mr. Martin. "Well, in that case, I'll help a little chap out."

Mr. Barlow hitched up his horse and put the big pane of glass in the wagon. They reached the house with the big pane all safe.

While Mr. Barlow put it in, Bobby stood watching him and looking at the clock every once in a while. When it was all done, he handed the four dollars to Mr. Barlow.

"And thank you ever so much for coming to-day," he said.

"It won't take as much as that," said the carpenter. And he handed a dollar back to Bobby.

"What time did you say Mother was coming?" he asked.

"On the four o'clock train," answered Bobby.

"There is time to wash it if you will bring the things," said Mr. Barlow.

Bobby washed the inside, while Mr. Barlow washed the outside.

And there was the Big Window, whole and bright and shiny again.

It was not long before Father and John came up to the house with Prince, to go to the train. Bobby and Sue and Betty all got into the carriage. Rover ran along beside it.

On the way to the station, Bobby told Father all about the window.

In a short time, the train came in sight down the track. In a few moments more, Bobby saw Mother coming from the train and ran to meet her.

And it was not long before she was home again, and they were all visiting together in the sitting-room.

As she sat in the big rocker near the window, Mother said, "I saw many beautiful sights on my trip, but none that I like better than the view from my beautiful, shiny, big window."

And then wasn't Bobby Hill happy!

XV

A few weeks after Mother came home, they were all gathered in the sitting-room after supper.

Outside, the rain beat against the window panes and the wind made a mournful sound among the evergreens.

Inside, all was bright and cheery. In the coal stove a fire was burning. On the table a big lamp sent a bright light through the room.

Baby Betty had been put to bed, but Bobby sat at the table, reading a new book.

"It is almost bedtime for you," said Mother.

"Can't we have a game of dominoes before I go?" asked Bobby.

Mother looked at the clock. "Just one," she said.

So they all gathered around the table in the center of the room—Father, Mother, John and Sue and Bobby.

Father and Bobby were partners. They got two hundred points first and so won the game.

When the game was over, John went down cellar and brought up a pan of apples. Bobby and Sue went to the attic and brought down a basin of walnuts. And as they were eating the walnuts and the apples, they had a merry time.

"I am glad we have such a comfortable place on this stormy night," said Mother.

"I always like our long Winter evenings," said Father.

Bobby was cracking nuts. Suddenly he stopped and listened to the rain.

"I hope the squirrels in the apple tree have plenty of nuts to-night," said he.

At half past eight, Bobby went upstairs to bed. Mother tucked him in and told him a good-night story. It was about Daniel in the Lion's Den that night.

When she came down, Father was reading his paper on one side of the table. Across from him, John sat reading a book. Sue was softly playing on the piano.

Mother stopped a moment in the doorway to enjoy the scene.

"Winter time or Summer time, home is best," she thought.

Then she took her place in the easy chair which John had drawn up for her near the lamp, and opened her book to read.

Upstairs, Bobby lay awake for some time, listening to the wind and rain.

Then he fell asleep and dreamed that he was in the hayfield playing with Rover; and the sound he heard was not the storm but the hum of the mower cutting the clover.

THE END

CPSIA information can be obtained
at www.ICGtesting.com
Printed in the USA
LVHW052356021121
702257LV00007B/856

9 789355 342768